1 SAMUEL
FROM START2FINISH

MICHAEL WHITWORTH

© 2025 by Start2Finish

All rights reserved. No part of this publication may be reproduced, stored in a retrieval system, or transmitted in any form or by any means without the prior written permission of the author. The only exception is brief quotations in printed reviews.

ISBN 978-1-944704-73-5

Published by Start2Finish
Bend, Oregon 97702
start2finish.org

Printed in the United States of America

Unless otherwise noted, all Scripture quotations are from The Holy Bible, English Standard Version®, copyright © 2001 by Crossway Bibles, a publishing ministry of Good News Publishers. Used by permission. All rights reserved.

Cover Design: Evangela Creative

CONTENTS

1.	Hannah's Prayer, Samuel's Call	5
2.	The Ark & God's Glory	11
3.	Israel Demands a King	17
4.	Samuel's Farewell Address	23
5.	Saul's Rash Choices	29
6.	Saul Rejected, David Anointed	35
7.	David & Goliath	41
8.	David's Rise, Saul's Jealousy	47
9.	David on the Run	53
10.	Sparing the Lord's Anointed	59
11.	Abigail's Wise Intervention	65
12.	David among the Philistines	71
13.	Saul's Final Night & Death	77

1

HANNAH'S PRAYER, SAMUEL'S CALL

1 SAMUEL 1–3

Objective: To show that God begins his redemptive work through weakness, prayer, and humble obedience rather than human power.

INTRODUCTION

The book of 1 Samuel begins in an unexpected way. Instead of trumpets announcing a king or soldiers rallying for battle, the opening scene focuses on a barren woman in tears. Hannah's emptiness mirrors Israel's national condition after the chaos of the book of Judges—hopeless, voiceless, and spiritually adrift. Yet it is in this very barrenness that God begins his work.

As we trace Hannah's story, Eli's decline, and Samuel's call, we see that God delights to work in weakness, reversals, and unlikely places. Israel's monarchy—and ultimately Christ himself—will not begin in the war room but in the prayer room.

EXAMINATION

Hannah's prayer of surrender (1:1–28)

The story opens with Elkanah and his two wives: Hannah, who is barren, and Peninnah, who taunts her mercilessly. Elkanah loves Hannah deeply but cannot understand her pain. His attempt to console her—"Am I not more to you than ten sons?"—only reveals how little he grasps her grief.

Childlessness in ancient Israel was not merely a private sorrow; it was seen as shame, even a curse. Hannah's anguish is sharpened each year as Peninnah mocks her. But in her desperation, Hannah turns to the Lord. She pours out her soul in prayer, asking for a son and vowing to dedicate him to the Lord's service.

This is the first great turning point. Hannah does not scheme, manipulate, or retaliate—she prays. Her vow is remarkable: she is ready to give back the very gift she longs for, living as if God has already answered. Prayer here is not bargaining but surrender.

When Eli, the priest, mistakes her prayer for drunkenness, it highlights his dull spiritual vision. Yet once corrected, he blesses her, and Hannah leaves comforted—not because her circumstances have changed, but because she has entrusted them to God. Soon the Lord "remembers" her, and Samuel is born, his very name meaning "heard by God."

Hannah's prayerful dependence sets the stage for the whole book. Israel's future will not come from clever politics or brute force, but from God's gracious intervention in response to humble prayer.

Hannah's song of reversal (2:1-11)

In chapter 2, Hannah breaks forth in praise. Her song moves beyond personal thanksgiving to a sweeping vision of God's character and rule. She exults that God humbles the proud and lifts the lowly, reverses fortunes, and establishes his kingdom.

This song is not just poetry—it is prophecy. It anticipates Israel's coming king, and ultimately Christ himself. Like Mary's Magnificat in Luke 1, Hannah's words proclaim that God is a God of great reversals. Where the world rewards pride and power, God exalts the humble and overturns the mighty.

Hannah's horn—her strength—has been lifted by God, and this becomes a lens through which we must read the rest of 1-2 Samuel. Every twist of Israel's story will demonstrate this truth: God rules history, not men.

Corruption in the priesthood (2:12-36)

The narrative then contrasts Hannah's faithfulness with the wickedness of Eli's sons, Hophni and Phinehas. Though priests, they are described as "worthless men" who abused their sacred office. They seized offerings by force, consumed what belonged to God, and even sexually exploited women serving at the tabernacle.

Eli rebukes them halfheartedly, but his failure to restrain them exposes his weakness as a leader. Worse still, he benefits from their corruption, enjoying the meat they stole. Their contempt for God's holiness is so severe that the Lord declares judgment: they will die, and Eli's priestly line will be cut off.

In sharp contrast, young Samuel grows "in stature and in favor with the Lord." Like a bright flower in a dunghill, Samuel's righteousness shines against the backdrop of spiritual rot.

This section is sobering. It warns us that spiritual privilege is no shield against judgment. To mishandle God's holiness is to invite his wrath. Yet it also comforts us that God is not thwarted by corrupt leaders—he raises up his own servants to accomplish his purposes.

Samuel's call and commission (3:1–21)

The story of Samuel's call is beloved in children's classes, yet its message is weighty. The chapter begins with the chilling note: "The word of the Lord was rare in those days." Spiritual famine hung over Israel. Eli, nearly blind, symbolizes the dimming light of Israel's priesthood. Yet "the lamp of God had not yet gone out"—a subtle hint of hope.

Three times Samuel hears God's voice and mistakes it for Eli's. Finally Eli realizes what is happening and instructs Samuel to respond: "Speak, Lord, for your servant hears."

The Lord delivers a devastating word: judgment is coming upon Eli's house, and no sacrifice can atone for their sin. Though young, Samuel faithfully reports this message. In doing so, he steps into the prophetic role, becoming the first national prophet since Moses.

From this moment on, "the Lord was with him," and "all Israel knew that Samuel was established as a prophet." The famine of God's word was over. The dawn had broken.

APPLICATION

1. God works through barrenness.

When life feels empty, hopeless, or barren, God is not absent. Hannah's story reminds us that barrenness does not mean abandonment. Sometimes God allows emptiness to prepare us for a greater work of his grace. In seasons when our strength is gone and our resources exhausted, we are positioned to depend wholly on him. Like Hannah, we may weep bitterly and feel forgotten, yet God often uses these very moments to show that his power is made perfect in weakness. Our barrenness may be the soil in which new life grows. When everything else fails, God remains faithful. In his time, he turns emptiness into joy, proving that despair never has the last word—grace does.

2. Prayer is power. Prayer changes us, and it shapes history.

Hannah teaches us that prayer is not a last resort but our first and best response. She poured out her soul with raw honesty, asking boldly yet surrendering completely. Her prayer did not just bring peace to her heart—it set in motion God's plan for Samuel, whose ministry shaped Israel's history. In the same way, prayer still has the power to transform our lives and the world around us. Prayer aligns us with God's purposes, lifts our burdens, and restores hope even before circumstances change. When we pray, we join our weakness to his strength. Prayer remains the believer's greatest weapon and the surest pathway to peace.

3. Leadership without holiness is ruin.

Ministry without integrity leads to disaster. The tragedy of Eli's sons warns us that religious activity is no substitute for a holy life. They wore priestly garments and handled sacred duties, yet their hearts were corrupt, and their ministry became a cloak for greed and lust. Eli himself allowed compromise to fester until judgment fell on his house. For us, this is a sobering reminder that leadership divorced from holiness is destined to collapse. God values integrity over image, faithfulness over appearance. Influence without obedience is a dangerous illusion. True leadership in God's kingdom flows from humility, purity, and devotion. When leaders walk closely with God, their service builds others up. Without holiness, ministry ruins everyone involved.

4. Hearing God's voice matters.

Our security lies not in cleverness but in responsiveness to God's Word.

Samuel's call shows us the importance of listening when God speaks. Unlike Eli's sons, who ignored every warning, Samuel responded with humility: "Speak, Lord, for your servant hears." This posture of openness became the foundation of his prophetic ministry. Today, God still speaks through his Word The challenge is whether we will listen. Clever strategies or human wisdom cannot replace obedience to God's voice. Security in life comes not from predicting the future or controlling outcomes, but from trusting and obeying the God who sees all. A receptive heart will always be safer than a brilliant mind closed to God's truth.

CONCLUSION

First Samuel 1–3 reminds us that God's story begins not with strength but with weakness, not with power but with prayer. Hannah's whispered petition, Eli's tragic blindness, and Samuel's prophetic call all weave together to show us the God who humbles the proud, exalts the lowly, and stubbornly pursues his purposes. In Christ, the true Prophet, Priest, and King, the dawn has broken over our barrenness. Our call is simple: pray, trust, obey—and watch the God of reversals at work.

REFLECTION

1. Why is Hannah's barrenness important to the story of Israel?

2. How did Hannah's prayer differ from mere bargaining with God?

3. What does Hannah's song (2:1–10) teach us about God's character?

4. How did Eli's sons abuse their role, and what was the consequence?

5. Why was Samuel's call such a turning point for Israel?

DISCUSSION

1. How does Hannah's perseverance in prayer encourage you in your struggles?

2. What practices help you cultivate a life of prayerful dependence on God?

3. In what ways can spiritual privilege become dangerous if divorced from obedience?

4. How can we discern God's voice today and remain responsive to his Word?

5. Where have you seen God bring life out of your own barrenness?

2

THE ARK & GOD'S GLORY
1 SAMUEL 4–7

Objective: To show that God's sovereign glory cannot be manipulated, only honored through repentance and obedience.

INTRODUCTION

Few stories in Scripture are more dramatic than the ark narrative in 1 Samuel 4–7. Israel faced crushing defeat, the ark was captured, and Eli's house collapsed. To the human eye, God's glory seemed gone. Yet in the darkness, he displayed his sovereignty—humbling Israel, humiliating Dagon, and thundering against the Philistines. These chapters remind us that God cannot be manipulated, domesticated, or reduced to a symbol. He is the ultimate heavyweight whose hand directs history. When his people repent and call on him, he brings victory and peace. The message is clear: God's presence is holy, his glory weighty, and his promises sure.

EXAMINATION

The ark misused and glory departed (4:1–22)

Israel faced the Philistines in battle at Ebenezer and suffered defeat, losing four thousand men. Rather than seeking God's word through Samuel, Israel's leaders presumed that bringing the ark into battle would guarantee victory. They treated the ark as a talisman rather than honoring the Lord of Hosts whom it represented. The result was catastrophic: 30,000 soldiers were slaughtered, Eli's corrupt sons were killed, and the ark itself was captured.

News of the ark's capture killed Eli, whose fall from his seat symbolized the end of his priestly rule. The birth of Ichabod, whose name means "no glory," summed up the despair—Israel believed the glory had departed. Yet this was not a failure of divine power but a display of divine judgment. God was disciplining his people for their sin.

Dagon humbled and the Philistines struck (5:1–12)

The Philistines carried the ark to Ashdod and placed it in the temple of Dagon as a trophy of victory. But the next morning Dagon's idol had toppled before the ark as though bowing in worship. When the idol was set back up, it fell again the next day, this time shattered with its head and hands severed. The God of Israel was declaring his supremacy over the gods of the nations.

Following this humiliation of Dagon, the Lord's hand grew heavy against Ashdod, Gath, and Ekron. The Philistines suffered plagues and panic wherever the ark went. What they thought was a prize turned out to be a curse. The true heavyweight was not Dagon but Yahweh, whose glory cannot be mocked.

The ark returned and reverence violated (6:1–21)

After seven months of devastation, the Philistines resolved to return the ark to Israel with a guilt offering of golden tumors and mice, symbols of the plague that had struck them. Two untrained cows were yoked to a new cart, and by God's providence they carried the ark straight to Beth-shemesh. The Philistines recognized that it was Yahweh's hand at work, even as Israel still failed to show proper reverence.

When the people of Beth-shemesh looked into the ark, they were struck down. Seventy men (some versions say 50,070) died because they treated the holiness of God lightly. Instead of repenting, they sought to send the ark away. The lesson is clear: God's presence is not to be trivialized. His glory is weighty and his holiness demands reverence.

Repentance, renewal, and the stone of help (7:1-17)

For twenty years Israel languished under Philistine oppression until Samuel called the nation to repentance. He urged them to put away idols and serve the Lord only. At Mizpah, the people confessed their sins, fasted, and offered sacrifice. When the Philistines attacked, Samuel prayed and God thundered from heaven, throwing the enemy into confusion.

Israel won a decisive victory and Samuel erected a stone called Ebenezer—"stone of help"—to commemorate God's deliverance. This was a turning point. Israel discovered that true security did not lie in symbols like the ark but in repentance, prayer, and obedience to Yahweh. The heavy hand of God that once brought judgment now brought salvation.

APPLICATION

1. Misplaced trust leads to disaster

Israel's greatest mistake at Ebenezer was confusing the ark with God himself. They thought his presence could be manipulated by carrying a box into battle. We face the same temptation when we reduce God to rituals, routines, or outward symbols—church buildings, religious habits, even ministry itself. These can point us to God but cannot replace him. Faith is not in the things of God but in God himself. When we trust in substitutes, we discover that our confidence is hollow. God cannot be used; he must be worshiped. True security comes from humble obedience and living faith, not outward signs.

2. God's glory is weighty and holy

The repeated theme of these chapters is the 'heaviness' of God's glory. When the ark was captured, Eli's daughter-in-law cried, "Ichabod—the glory has departed." Yet God was not defeated; his glory was revealing itself in judgment and deliverance. To take God lightly is lethal, as Beth-shemesh learned. His presence demands reverence, not casual familiarity. In worship, prayer, and daily life, we must remember we approach the Holy One. Reverence means treating him with weight—giving him honor, priority, and obedience. The God of glory is not to be managed but magnified, not trivialized but treasured.

3. God cannot be contained or controlled

The Philistines thought they had captured Israel's God, and Israel thought they could wield him like a weapon. Both learned the same lesson: God is free, sovereign, and untamable. We may try to fit him into our agendas or bend him to our plans, but God will not be boxed in. He is not a charm to secure success, nor a servant of our ambitions. His hand directs history, often in ways that overturn our expectations. Faith means surrendering to his freedom, trusting his wisdom, and yielding our will. God's sovereignty is not a threat but a comfort, for his power works for the good of his people.

4. Repentance brings renewal

For twenty years, Israel lived in defeat until they turned back to God with confession, fasting, and sacrifice. Samuel's intercession and their repentance led to God's thunderous deliverance and lasting peace. The turning point was not the return of the ark but the return of the people's hearts to God. This remains true today. Renewal in our churches and lives does not begin with better strategies or stronger leaders but with repentance—honest confession, idol removal, and wholehearted devotion. God is ready to restore when his people return. Repentance may be painful, but it always opens the way for God's mercy and power to flow.

CONCLUSION

The ark narrative shows us that God is holy, weighty, and sovereign. He disciplines his people when they treat him lightly, yet he never abandons them. Through repentance and intercession, he restores and delivers. The Philistines trembled, Israel stumbled, but Samuel's leadership brought renewal through prayer and obedience. Our call is to honor God's glory, trust his sovereignty, and return to him in repentance. For the God who humbled Dagon, struck Philistia, and thundered at Mizpah is the same God who reigns today. To take him lightly is death, but to give him weight is life.

REFLECTION

1. What mistake did Israel make in bringing the ark into battle?

2. How did God demonstrate his power over Dagon and the Philistines?

3. Why was Beth-shemesh judged for looking into the ark?

4. What was the significance of Samuel's intercession at Mizpah?

5. What did Samuel name the stone he erected and what did the name mean?

DISCUSSION

1. How are we tempted to trust religious symbols instead of God himself?

2. How can we avoid trying to "box God in" with our own agendas?

3. What does it mean to give God the "weight" he deserves in your life?

4. Why is repentance essential for renewal, both personally and in the church?

5. Where do you see God's heavy hand at work today—in discipline, deliverance, or both?

3

ISRAEL DEMANDS A KING
1 SAMUEL 8–10

Objectives: To show that trusting human strength over God's rule leads to loss, but his sovereignty still prepares Christ's reign.

INTRODUCTION

Israel's demand for a king in 1 Samuel 8–10 is one of the most striking examples of rejecting God while thinking they were securing their future. They had just seen God thunder against the Philistines without a king, yet they still insisted on a human monarch. The irony is sharp: they wanted security, but in demanding a king like the nations, they invited slavery. These chapters warn us about the cost of trusting in appearances and human power rather than God. At the same time, they reveal God's providence in raising up Saul—and beyond him, preparing the way for Christ, the true King.

EXAMINATION

Israel's rejection of God's kingship (8:1–22)

The story of Israel's monarchy begins with a tragic irony. After Samuel grew old, his corrupt sons failed to walk in his ways. Rather than trusting God to provide leadership, Israel's elders demanded a king. Their reasoning was deeply flawed: they claimed to reject dynastic corruption by asking for a monarchy that would itself be dynastic.

At the heart of their demand was unbelief—wanting to be like the nations rather than set apart for God (8:20). The issue was not that kingship itself was forbidden. Deuteronomy 17 anticipated a king but placed strict conditions on his character: he must not amass wealth, wives, or horses, and he must humbly obey God's law. Israel's sin was not desiring a king but desiring the wrong kind of king. They sought conformity with the world instead of covenant faithfulness to God.

Samuel was grieved, perceiving their demand as evil. Yet when he prayed, God told him to obey the people's voice. This was not God's endorsement but his discipline—sometimes he gives us what we ask for so that we can learn from the consequences. God reminded Samuel that Israel's rejection was not personal but aimed at the Lord: they had forsaken God as their King. This had been their pattern since Egypt, repeatedly turning to idols and earthly rulers. By demanding a king, Israel was not simply requesting new leadership; they were rejecting God's kingship over them.

Samuel warned the people that kings take: sons for armies, daughters for labor, land, crops, and freedom. The repeated verb "take" dominates his speech, highlighting how rulers drain their people. Israel wanted protection, but Samuel warned they would find only oppression. Most sobering was the warning that one day they would cry out under their king's rule, but the Lord would not answer (8:18). Still, the people refused to listen. They wanted a king at any cost, even if it meant forfeiting their unique identity as God's chosen people.

Saul: The king israel wanted (9:1-10:27)

These chapters introduce Saul, Israel's first monarch. Outwardly, Saul looked the part. He came from a wealthy family and was the tallest, most handsome man in Israel. But the narrator hints at weaknesses beneath the surface. He was unable to find his father's donkeys, needed his servant's prompting to seek the prophet, and did not even know who Samuel was—astonishing given Samuel's fame throughout Israel. These details foreshadow Saul's lack of spiritual depth and initiative. His impressive stature masked an insecure heart. Yet God's providence guided every step of Saul's journey to Samuel, showing that the Lord remained sovereign even in Israel's misguided request. God would use Saul to discipline his people and prepare the way for David.

When Samuel anointed Saul, God confirmed his choice with three signs: the donkeys were found, strangers gave Saul bread, and a band of prophets caused Saul to prophesy by the Spirit. Each sign underscored that Saul's success would depend on God's power, not his own strength. The Spirit rushed upon Saul, equipping him to lead, but the change was temporary and conditional on obedience. Instead of stepping forward in faith, Saul hesitated. When chosen by lot before the people, he was hiding among the baggage. Outwardly impressive, inwardly fearful, Saul embodied Israel's misplaced values. They wanted a king like the nations, and that is exactly what they got—a man who looked strong but proved spiritually fragile.

Theologically, these chapters confront us with three realities. First, God's people often crave visible substitutes for invisible trust. Israel thought a human king would secure them, just as we often trust money, politics, or status to give us safety. Such substitutes reveal unbelief.

Second, appearances deceive. Saul looked like a king, but true leadership is measured by obedience to God. God had defined kingship in Deuteronomy 17, stressing humility and devotion to his Word, but Israel's choice was driven by sight, not faith.

Third, God remains sovereign even over human folly. Israel's sinful demand did not thwart his plan. He used Saul to teach them the cost of misplaced trust while preparing David, and ultimately Christ, the King after his own heart. What Israel wanted and what they needed were two different things. God gave them Saul, but he was already preparing the true King who would not take but give himself for his people. The warning is timeless: when we clamor for substitutes to replace God, he may allow us to taste their emptiness. Yet his purposes always move forward toward Christ, the King we truly need.

APPLICATION

1. Beware of wanting the wrong things

Israel's demand for a king warns us about confusing wants with needs. They wanted a king like the nations, but what they truly needed was trust in God as their King. We often repeat their mistake. We crave visible assurances—financial security, human approval, or political leaders who promise a better future. Yet these substitutes always disappoint. When we elevate our desires above God's wisdom, he may let us taste the fruit of those choices—not to destroy us, but to teach us that our deepest need is him. True security comes not from getting what we want but from trusting the God who knows what we need.

2. God sometimes gives us what we ask for

When Israel insisted on having a king, God told Samuel to give them one. This was not approval but discipline. In his sovereignty, God sometimes grants our misguided requests to teach us hard lessons. We may long for things that are not ultimately good for us—relationships, ambitions, or possessions that seem appealing but leave us empty. When God allows us to have them, it is to reveal their emptiness and drive us back to him. The painful fruit of wrong desires can be a mercy if it reminds us of our true need. God's discipline is never to destroy, but to restore us to himself.

3. Appearances can deceive

Saul looked like the perfect choice. He was tall, handsome, and impressive to the eye. Yet beneath the surface lay fear, hesitancy, and spiritual shallowness. Israel judged by appearances and got exactly what they asked for. We are tempted to do the same—evaluating leaders, opportunities, or even ourselves by what looks impressive on the outside. But God looks at the heart. Outward strength and image cannot replace inward faith and obedience. The lesson is clear: don't be fooled by appearances. What matters most is character shaped by God's Word and Spirit. Faithfulness, not flashiness, is what God values in his servants.

4. Christ is the King we need

Every human ruler takes, but Christ gives. Samuel warned that kings would seize sons, daughters, land, and freedom. That prophecy came true in Saul and in every monarch who followed. Yet Jesus came not to take but to give—his life, his righteousness, his Spirit. He is the only King who satisfies because he is the King we were made for. Israel's failure under Saul highlights our need for a perfect King. Human leaders will fail us, but Christ reigns forever in justice and mercy. Our response should not be to clamor for substitutes but to gladly submit to the King who gives himself for us.

CONCLUSION

Israel's demand for a king exposed their unbelief and misplaced trust. They traded the invisible rule of God for the visible image of Saul, a man who looked strong but proved weak. Yet even in their failure, God remained sovereign, using Saul to prepare for David and David to point to Christ.

The lesson is timeless: human rulers take, but Christ gives. Our call is to trust God's wisdom, not our desires, and to submit to the true King whose reign brings life and peace.

REFLECTION

1. Why was Israel's demand for a king sinful?
2. What did Samuel warn that kings would do?
3. How did Saul's appearance contrast with his character?
4. What role did God's providence play in Saul's rise?
5. How do these chapters point forward to Christ?

DISCUSSION

1. When are you tempted to trust substitutes instead of God?
2. How can we guard against judging by outward appearances?
3. Have you experienced God giving you what you asked for to teach you a lesson? How so?
4. What makes Christ's kingship different from every human ruler?
5. How can we live daily in submission to Christ as King?

4

SAMUEL'S FAREWELL ADDRESS
1 SAMUEL 11-12

Objectives: To show that true security rests not in kings or strength, but in God's Spirit and faithfulness.

INTRODUCTION

The opening chapters of Saul's reign bring both triumph and warning. In chapter 11, Saul led Israel to a decisive victory over the Ammonites, proving himself as a military leader. But in chapter 12, Samuel reminded the people that their demand for a king was rooted in unbelief. The prophet's farewell address sounded more like a courtroom than a celebration—he vindicated his own integrity, rehearsed Israel's history of rebellion, and warned that their future depended on fearing and obeying the Lord. These chapters teach us that human leaders rise and fall, but God's covenant faithfulness remains the sure foundation for his people.

EXAMINATION

Saul's victory over the Ammonites (11:1–15)

The Ammonite crisis in chapter 11 sets the stage for Saul's first test as king. Nahash, whose name fittingly means "snake," besieged Jabesh-gilead and demanded the gouging out of every man's right eye as the price of surrender. This humiliation would have crippled the city militarily and disgraced Israel nationally. The elders of Jabesh-gilead, paralyzed by fear, sought a treaty instead of seeking the Lord. Their despair illustrates a familiar danger—when we stop praying in faith, we surrender in fear before the battle even begins.

When Saul heard the news, the Spirit of God rushed upon him. Filled with righteous anger, he rallied Israel with a dramatic gesture: he cut an ox into pieces and sent them throughout the land as a summons to arms. The dread of the Lord fell on the people, and Israel united under Saul's leadership. At dawn, Saul's forces struck the Ammonites and achieved a decisive victory. The people acclaimed Saul as king, and his coronation at Gilgal marked a moment of national unity. Yet Saul himself deflected glory from himself to the Lord, recognizing that salvation belonged to God (11:13). This episode established Saul as God's instrument of deliverance, though it also raised the deeper question: if God had given victory through his Spirit, why had Israel clamored for a king at all?

Samuel's farewell and God's faithfulness (12:1–25)

That question is addressed in chapter 12, where Samuel delivered his farewell address. Like Moses and Joshua before him, Samuel reminded the people of God's past faithfulness. But unlike those earlier speeches, his words carried a sharp rebuke. First, Samuel vindicated his integrity. Unlike the kings of the nations, he had never taken from the people—not bribes, not property, not even an ox or donkey. The contrast was intentional: human kings take, but God's servants give. The people affirmed Samuel's innocence, clearing the way for his prosecution of their sin.

Samuel then rehearsed Israel's history. From the Exodus through the time of the judges, God had repeatedly delivered his people when they cried out to him. Never once had he failed them. Their demand for a king, therefore, was not a solution to insecurity but an act of rebellion. They had feared Nahash more than they trusted Yahweh. Samuel's words cut to the heart: their problem was not external enemies but internal unbelief. Leadership structures would not save them; only covenant faithfulness to God could.

The climax of Samuel's speech came with a sign. Calling on the Lord, he summoned thunder and rain during the wheat harvest—a season when storms were unheard of. The sudden storm confirmed that their demand for a king was evil in God's sight. The people trembled and begged Samuel to intercede for them. Samuel did not minimize their sin—he bluntly told them, "You have done all this evil" (12:20). Yet he also offered hope: if they feared the Lord and served him faithfully, God would not abandon them. Why? Because of his great name and his determination to make them his people (12:22). God's faithfulness was not grounded in their performance but in his own reputation and covenant love.

Samuel concluded with both comfort and warning. He pledged to continue praying for Israel and teaching them the good and right way, setting a pattern for prophets to come. But he also warned that if they persisted in evil, both they and their king would be swept away. The thunderstorm pointed forward to exile, when rebellion would finally result in judgment. Even so, Samuel's words ultimately direct us to Christ. Like Samuel, Jesus vindicated his integrity before hostile crowds. Like Samuel, he prayed for his people. But unlike Samuel, Jesus bore the judgment of exile himself, cut off on the cross so that his people might never be abandoned. In him, God's faithfulness finds its fullest expression. Israel demanded a king, but what they truly needed was the King of kings—faithful, merciful, and eternal.

APPLICATION

1. God's Spirit empowers courage

When Saul heard of Jabesh-gilead's plight, it was the Spirit of God that transformed him from a hesitant farmer into a bold leader. Fear turned to resolve, and disunity turned to unity because God's power was at work. The same Spirit still empowers believers today. Courage is not the absence of fear but confidence in God's presence. Like Saul, we face battles that seem overwhelming, yet God equips his people for the task. We should not shrink back in despair but step forward in faith, trusting that the Spirit who emboldened Saul and the apostles will also strengthen us for our callings.

2. God's servants give, not take

Samuel contrasted his life with the abuses of earthly kings. He had never exploited the people or enriched himself at their expense. In a world where leaders often take—draining resources, demanding loyalty, and abusing authority—God calls his servants to give. True leadership is marked by integrity, humility, and generosity. In our families, workplaces, and churches, we must resist the temptation to use others for our gain. Instead, we should imitate Christ, who came not to be served but to serve. Leadership in God's kingdom is not about taking advantage of others but about laying down our lives for them.

3. Sin is real, but so is grace

When Israel realized their sin in demanding a king, they begged Samuel to pray for them. His response was blunt: "You have done all this evil." Yet he did not leave them in despair. He pointed them to God's faithfulness, rooted in his great name. The same is true for us. We cannot deny or minimize our sin, but neither should we be crushed by it. God's grace is greater than our failures. The gospel reminds us that Christ bore our guilt and intercedes for us even now. Sin is serious, but grace is stronger. Our hope is not in our record but in God's unshakable faithfulness.

4. Faithfulness is the path of life

Samuel told Israel that obedience would bring blessing, while rebellion would bring destruction. The same principle still applies. Faithfulness is not about earning God's love but about living in alignment with his will. When we walk in obedience, we experience his peace, joy, and protection. When we rebel, we reap sorrow and discipline. The choice before Israel is the choice before us: serve the Lord wholeheartedly or chase empty things that cannot save. Christ has already secured our salvation, but daily faithfulness keeps us close to him. The path of life is marked by reverence, trust, and steadfast obedience.

CONCLUSION

In 1 Samuel 11–12, Saul tasted victory, but Samuel reminded Israel that their security rested not in kings but in God. The thunderstorm at harvest testified to the seriousness of their sin, yet Samuel pointed them to God's unshakable faithfulness. These chapters teach us that sin is real, but grace is greater; human leaders may falter, but God's covenant never fails. Our response is to fear the Lord, trust his promises, and walk faithfully in his ways. For in Christ, the true King and eternal Intercessor, God's salvation is secure forever.

REFLECTION

1. What was Nahash's demand of Jabesh-gilead, and why was it significant?

2. How did the Spirit of God empower Saul's leadership in chapter 11?

3. Why did Samuel vindicate his integrity before addressing Israel's sin?

4. What was the meaning of the thunderstorm during the wheat harvest?

5. How does Samuel point Israel to both warning and hope in chapter 12?

DISCUSSION

1. What fears tempt us to surrender rather than trust God?

2. How can we embody leadership that gives rather than takes?

3. Where have you experienced God's grace meeting your sin?

4. What "empty things" tempt us to turn aside from wholehearted obedience?

5. How does Christ fulfill the role of true King and Intercessor for us today?

5

SAUL'S RASH CHOICES
1 SAMUEL 13–14

Objectives: To show that God desires wholehearted obedience and faith, not outward religion or empty appearances of devotion.

INTRODUCTION

Saul's reign began with promise, but by chapters 13–14, cracks in his leadership are unmistakable. He looked the part of a king, but his heart was not surrendered to God. These chapters contrast two men: Saul, who relied on appearances and rash vows, and Jonathan, who trusted the Lord with bold faith. Together they reveal that God desires not religious gestures or empty rituals, but hearts that obey him fully. The story warns us that faith without obedience is hollow, and that true strength lies not in strategy or image, but in reliance on God.

EXAMINATION

The events of 1 Samuel 13–14 highlight the widening gap between Saul's outward religion and his inward disobedience. He continued to perform sacrifices, speak God's name, and make vows, but beneath the surface his actions revealed fear, pride, and a lack of surrender. These chapters show that God is not impressed by religious appearances. What he desires is obedience flowing from faith.

Saul's disobedience at Gilgal (13:1-23)

In chapter 13, the Philistines gathered at Michmash with a massive army, including thousands of chariots and horsemen. Samuel had commanded Saul to wait seven days at Gilgal for his arrival to offer sacrifices. The command was clear: wait. But as Israel's troops grew restless and many deserted, Saul panicked. Rather than trusting God's word, he offered the burnt offering himself. To outsiders, it may have looked like an act of piety. But God saw it as presumption. Saul attempted to secure God's favor while disobeying God's word. Samuel's rebuke was sharp: because Saul had not kept the Lord's command, his kingdom would not endure. God was seeking a man after his own heart who would obey him fully. This was more than a ritual mistake; it exposed Saul's heart—a leader more concerned with appearances than obedience.

Jonathan's faith and Saul's folly (14:1-52)

The narrative contrasts Saul's fear with Jonathan's faith. In chapter 14, Jonathan and his armor-bearer slipped away from camp to attack a Philistine outpost. His reasoning was simple yet profound: "The Lord can save by many or by few." Jonathan believed that victory did not depend on numbers or weapons but on God's power. Climbing a steep ravine, the two men attacked, killing twenty soldiers. Panic spread through the Philistine camp, and even an earthquake confirmed that God was fighting for Israel. Jonathan's trust sparked deliverance for the nation. The contrast could not be clearer: while Saul cowered in hesitation, his son moved forward in faith, and God acted mightily.

But Saul's failures did not end at Gilgal. Even in the midst of Jonathan's God-given victory, Saul's rash leadership nearly ruined everything. He placed his army under a foolish oath, forbidding them to eat until evening. His motive was selfish—he wanted vengeance on "my enemies." The oath weakened his soldiers, robbed them of strength, and led them into sin when they slaughtered animals and ate the blood. Jonathan, unaware of the command, ate honey and was refreshed. Instead of rejoicing in God's provision, Saul was ready to execute his son to preserve his vow.

Only the intervention of the people spared Jonathan's life. The incident revealed Saul's distorted priorities: he prized his image and rash words above the well-being of his people and the will of God.

The summary at the end of chapter 14 underscores the narrator's verdict. Though Saul fought battles against Israel's enemies and enjoyed some success, his reign is described as one of constant struggle. Unlike the summaries of David's reign, there is no mention that the Lord gave Saul victory wherever he went. The theological point is clear: leadership without obedience is failure. Saul may have looked impressive and achieved temporary victories, but he did not walk faithfully with God. His reign was marked more by fear, folly, and frustration than by faithfulness.

Several lessons stand out from these chapters. First, obedience matters more than appearances. Saul went through religious motions but disobeyed God's command.

Second, faith trusts God's power above human strength. Jonathan acted boldly because he knew God was able to save.

Third, rash words and prideful vows lead to ruin. Saul's foolish oath nearly cost Israel its victory and Jonathan his life.

Finally, God's purposes advance despite failed leaders. Saul's shortcomings prepared the way for David, the man after God's heart, and ultimately for Christ, the perfect King whose obedience secures salvation for his people.

The story of Saul and Jonathan reminds us that appearances can be deceiving. Saul looked like a king, but Jonathan acted like a man of faith. In the end, what matters most is not how impressive we seem but whether our hearts are surrendered to God. Saul sought control, recognition, and personal vengeance; Jonathan sought the glory of God. God honored Jonathan's trust but rejected Saul's pride. For us, the choice is the same: will we cling to appearances and empty gestures, or will we trust and obey the Lord with all our hearts?

APPLICATION

1. Obedience is better than appearances

Saul performed the sacrifice at Gilgal because he feared losing his troops more than disobeying God. Outwardly, it looked like devotion; inwardly, it revealed unbelief. This warns us against settling for religious appearances without surrendered hearts. We can attend services, pray, or even serve in ministry while still refusing to obey God in areas that cost us. True faith is proven not by gestures but by obedience. God is not impressed with rituals that mask rebellion. He desires our hearts, our trust, and our willingness to follow his Word even when circumstances seem overwhelming. To obey is better than sacrifice, because obedience flows from genuine love and faith.

2. Faith acts boldly in God's power

Jonathan's assault on the Philistine garrison reminds us that true faith does not wait for ideal circumstances. He believed God could save whether by many or by few, and that conviction gave him courage to act. Faith does not eliminate risk, but it trusts God's sovereignty above the odds. Like Jonathan, we may face battles that seem impossible. Faith calls us to move forward in obedience, trusting that God's power is greater than our weakness. Bold faith inspires others, as Jonathan's courage rallied Israel. When we live with that kind of trust, we become instruments through which God displays his strength and glory.

3. Beware of rash words and vows

Saul's oath that no soldier could eat until evening was not piety but pride. It weakened his men, endangered victory, and nearly cost Jonathan his life. Rash words often reveal hearts seeking control rather than surrender. We, too, may speak in haste—making promises to manipulate outcomes, impress others, or cover our insecurity. But words spoken without wisdom or submission to God bring harm. Scripture warns us to be slow to speak and careful with our commitments (Jas. 1:19; Eph. 5:2). Instead of rash vows, God calls us to steady obedience and humble prayer. True devotion is not found in dramatic statements but in quiet, consistent trust.

4. God's purposes prevail despite failed leaders

Saul's reign is a sobering reminder that leadership without obedience falters. Yet even Saul's failures could not derail God's plan. Through Jonathan's faith and later through David's rise, God advanced his purposes. This truth comforts us when leaders fail today. God is not dependent on human perfection to accomplish his will. He remains faithful even when people falter.

For believers, this points us to Christ, the perfect King who never fails, whose obedience secures our salvation. When human leaders disappoint, we look to the One whose reign is eternal, whose promises are sure, and whose purposes cannot be thwarted.

CONCLUSION

In 1 Samuel 13–14, Saul's rashness and disobedience exposed his heart, while Jonathan's faith revealed what God desires—a heart that trusts and obeys. Religious appearances could not save Saul, and rash vows nearly cost him everything. Yet God's purposes continued, paving the way for a king after his own heart. The lesson is clear: obedience is greater than ritual, faith is stronger than fear, and God's plans are never thwarted. In Christ, the true King, we find the perfect obedience that brings salvation and the faithfulness that secures our hope.

REFLECTION

1. What did Saul do wrong at Gilgal, and why was it serious?
2. How did Jonathan's faith contrast with Saul's fear?
3. What consequences came from Saul's rash vow?
4. Why does God value obedience more than ritual sacrifices?
5. How do these chapters prepare for David and point to Christ?

DISCUSSION

1. Where are you tempted to trust appearances instead of obeying God?
2. How can Jonathan's faith inspire boldness in your own walk with God?
3. What are examples of rash words or vows we should avoid today?
4. How do we respond when leaders fail us spiritually or morally?
5. How does Christ's obedience secure hope when ours falters?

6

SAUL REJECTED, DAVID ANOINTED

1 SAMUEL 15-16

Objective: To show that God rejects partial obedience and outward religion, choosing hearts fully devoted to his will.

INTRODUCTION

First Samuel 15–16 stands as one of the most pivotal moments in Israel's history. Saul, the king chosen at the people's request, is decisively rejected because of his repeated disobedience. The command to devote Amalek to destruction was clear, yet Saul spared what was valuable and justified his actions. Samuel confronted him with the timeless truth: "To obey is better than sacrifice." In the wake of Saul's rejection, God sent Samuel to Bethlehem to anoint David, the shepherd boy who would become king. These chapters remind us that God values obedience above appearances and that his purposes move forward through his chosen servant.

EXAMINATION

Saul's disobedience and rejection (15:1–35)

The command to destroy Amalek in chapter 15 reaches back centuries to Israel's first battle after leaving Egypt (Exod. 17). The Amalekites had attacked Israel's stragglers with cruelty, and God swore that he would be at war with Amalek from generation to generation. Deuteronomy 25 reinforced the command to blot out Amalek's memory once Israel had rest in the land. Saul, therefore, was not given an arbitrary task but a sacred duty to carry out God's justice. The order was explicit: devote everything to destruction—men, women, children, livestock—nothing was to remain. This practice, called *hērem*, meant complete dedication to God by destruction, a recognition that the battle was his, not Israel's.

At first, Saul appeared obedient. He gathered his troops and struck Amalek "from Havilah to Shur." But the narrator makes clear that Saul failed to obey fully. He spared King Agag and the best of the livestock, destroying only what was worthless. This partial obedience was, in truth, disobedience. God declared to Samuel, "I regret that I have made Saul king." While God does not change his eternal purposes, the language conveys divine grief at human rebellion. Samuel was also grieved, crying out to the Lord all night. The prophet felt the weight of Saul's failure and the devastation it would bring to Israel.

When Samuel confronted Saul, the king greeted him with self-deception: "I have carried out the Lord's instructions." But the bleating of sheep and the lowing of oxen betrayed him. Saul shifted blame to the people, claiming they spared the best animals to sacrifice to God. Yet such sacrifices were illegitimate—the spoil already belonged to God under the ban. Saul was not giving God a gift; he was stealing from him. Samuel exposed Saul's manipulation: he wanted the appearance of obedience without the reality. The prophet's words cut to the heart: "Does the Lord delight in burnt offerings and sacrifices as much as in obeying the Lord? To obey is better than sacrifice."

Samuel compared Saul's rebellion to witchcraft and idolatry. Disobedience, at its core, places self above God and elevates personal will over divine command. For this reason, Saul's kingship was rejected. Though Saul mouthed repentance, it was shallow. He admitted fault only after repeated confrontation and remained more concerned with appearances before the elders than with true humility before God. Even his request for Samuel to honor him showed his fixation on reputation. The tearing of Samuel's robe became a sign: God had torn the kingdom from Saul and given it to a better man.

Samuel carried out what Saul would not, executing Agag and fulfilling God's justice. Afterward, Samuel and Saul parted ways, never to see each other again. The chapter closes in grief—Samuel mourning, God grieving, but Saul unrepentant. The tragedy is palpable: Saul had begun with promise, but pride and disobedience ended his reign. The chapter underscores the covenant truth that obedience is the heart of worship, and rebellion is treason against God's kingship.

David's anointing and God's choice of the heart (16:1-23)
Chapter 16 shifts from rejection to hope. God rebuked Samuel for mourning and sent him to Bethlehem to anoint a new king. At Jesse's house, Samuel was impressed with Eliab's stature, but God corrected him: "Man looks on the outward appearance, but the Lord looks on the heart" (16:7). One by one, Jesse's sons passed, but none were chosen. Finally, David, the youngest and least likely, was summoned from the fields. When Samuel anointed him, the Spirit of the Lord rushed upon David from that day forward. Unlike Saul, whose anointing was temporary and conditional, David received the Spirit's enduring presence. The shepherd boy, overlooked by men, was chosen by God to be king.

The chapter concludes with a striking irony. As God's Spirit came upon David, it departed from Saul. In its place, a harmful spirit tormented the rejected king. Saul's servants sought relief through music, and David was brought to play the lyre. Unbeknownst to Saul, he welcomed into his service the very one who would replace him. The rejected king was soothed by the presence of the anointed king, even as the reader sees God's providence unfolding. What began in Saul's disobedience now turns toward God's chosen ruler, a man after his heart. These chapters remind us that human leaders fail, but God's plans prevail, and his choice rests not on outward greatness but on inward devotion.

APPLICATION

1. Partial obedience is disobedience

Saul obeyed only halfway. He attacked Amalek but spared Agag and the best animals. In doing so, he revealed that his standard was convenience, not God's command. Partial obedience is really disobedience, because it substitutes our judgment for God's authority. We may think compromise is harmless, but God sees it as rebellion. The principle applies today: selective obedience in worship, morality, or service is unacceptable. God desires complete devotion, not half-measures. When we obey fully, we declare that God's wisdom is greater than our own. Obedience may be costly, but disobedience always costs more. The lesson is clear: God is honored by wholehearted trust, not partial compliance.

2. Obedience is better than sacrifice

Samuel's words to Saul are timeless: God values obedience more than ritual. The nations thought sacrifices sustained their gods, but Israel's God needs nothing. What he desires is hearts aligned with his will. Saul tried to mask rebellion with offerings, but God saw through it. The same danger exists today. We may rely on religious practices—attendance, giving, service—while ignoring God's call to holiness and repentance. But worship without obedience is empty. True sacrifice is a life surrendered to God's will. The gospel calls us not to manipulate God with rituals but to yield our hearts in faith and love. Obedience is the highest form of worship.

3. God looks at the heart

When Samuel saw Eliab, he assumed the eldest and strongest son was God's choice. But God rejected appearances and chose David, the overlooked shepherd boy. This reveals a principle that still stands: God values inward devotion over outward impressiveness. Our culture prizes charisma, image, and status, but God's eyes penetrate deeper. He seeks humility, integrity, and faith. This truth both humbles and comforts us. It humbles because we cannot impress God with outward show. It comforts because no one is too small, too hidden, or too ordinary for God to use. What he desires is a heart fully yielded to him.

4. God's purposes prevail despite human failure

Saul's failure did not derail God's plan. Though Israel's first king fell short, God was already raising up David. This truth gives us confidence in times of disappointment. Leaders may fail, institutions may falter, but God's purposes march on. He works through weakness, rejection, and even rebellion to bring about his will. The cross itself is the greatest example—what seemed like defeat became victory. For believers, this truth anchors our hope. We need not fear when circumstances crumble, because God remains sovereign. Our call is to trust his unfolding plan and rest in his promise that he is always working for our good and his glory.

CONCLUSION

First Samuel 15–16 marks the transition from Saul's failed reign to David's anointed kingship. Saul's partial obedience exposed his rebellion, and God's rejection was final. Yet God's purposes did not end with Saul. In David, God raised up a man after his own heart, one whose anointing pointed forward to Christ, the true King. These chapters teach us that obedience matters, appearances deceive, and God's plan cannot be stopped. Our response is to yield fully to God, trust his wisdom, and take comfort that his purposes always prevail.

REFLECTION

1. Why was Saul's treatment of Amalek considered disobedience?
2. What does the principle "to obey is better than sacrifice" mean?
3. How did Saul reveal his concern for appearances rather than repentance?
4. Why was David chosen over Eliab and his brothers?
5. How do these chapters highlight God's sovereignty despite human failure?

DISCUSSION

1. Where are we tempted to offer God partial obedience?
2. How do we sometimes substitute ritual for genuine obedience?
3. What encourages you about God's choice of David, the least likely son?
4. How does God's sovereignty comfort you when leaders fail or circumstances disappoint?
5. In what ways does Christ fulfill the picture of the obedient and anointed King?

7

DAVID & GOLIATH
1 SAMUEL 17

Objective: To show that God wins victory through his anointed servant, displaying power through weakness and faith, not strength.

INTRODUCTION

Few stories in the Bible are as well-known as David and Goliath, yet few are as often misunderstood. This is not just a tale of underdog triumph or self-help inspiration. The real message is about God's power to deliver through his anointed servant. The battle in the valley of Elah was not won by superior weapons or skill, but by faith in the God who saves "not with sword and spear." In David's victory, we see not merely bravery but theology—God shaming human strength through weakness. This story ultimately points beyond David to Christ, the greater Son of David, who defeated the ultimate giant: sin and death.

EXAMINATION

Goliath's challenge and Israel's fear (17:1–11)

The setting is the valley of Elah in the Shephelah, the lowland region between Judah and Philistia. Here, armies of Israel and the Philistines faced off, separated by a dry wadi. Out from the Philistine camp emerged Goliath of Gath, a warrior of staggering size—nearly ten feet tall—armed with massive armor and weapons. His very appearance inspired terror. He mocked Israel, demanding champion warfare: one-on-one combat to determine the fate of the nations. This was common in the ancient world, but the stakes were high. For forty days, Goliath taunted Israel, and for forty days Saul and his army trembled. The king who stood head and shoulders above the people (10:23) hid behind them, powerless without the Spirit of God that had once empowered him.

David's faith and conviction (17:12-37)

Into this paralysis stepped David, the youngest son of Jesse, who arrived bringing food to his brothers. David heard Goliath's taunts and was indignant. To him, this was not just a military threat but blasphemy: an uncircumcised Philistine defying the armies of the living God. David's words reveal his perspective of faith. Where Israel's soldiers saw size and strength, David saw covenant weakness. Goliath did not belong to God's people, and therefore he had no ultimate power. David's confidence came not from youthful arrogance but from a theological conviction: God's honor was at stake, and God would act.

When David volunteered to fight, Saul doubted him, pointing out his youth and inexperience. David countered with testimony from his life as a shepherd. God had delivered him from lions and bears, and he would deliver him from this Philistine. The key was not David's past skill but God's faithfulness. Saul attempted to equip David with his armor, perhaps hoping to share in the credit, but David refused. He had not tested the armor, and more importantly, he wanted it clear that victory would come not by human means but by God's power. Armed only with a sling and five smooth stones, David stepped onto the battlefield as the least likely champion.

The battle belongs to the Lord (17:41-58)

As Goliath advanced, mocking David and cursing God, David responded with one of the most theologically rich declarations in Scripture. He proclaimed that the Lord would deliver Goliath into his hand, not so that David would gain glory, but so that all the earth would know there is a God in Israel. He insisted that the Lord saves "not with sword and spear," for the battle belongs to the Lord (17:47). This speech is the heart of the chapter. It explains the meaning of the victory before the battle even takes place. David was not trusting his aim or his sling; he was trusting the God who delivers.

When the moment came, David ran toward Goliath. With a single stone, he struck the giant in the forehead, felling him face down, just as Dagon had fallen before the ark. David then took Goliath's own sword and cut off his head. The Philistines fled in panic, and Israel pursued in triumph. The narrator underscores the miracle: "There was no sword in the hand of David" (17:50). The victory was not due to human might or weapons, but to the power of God working through weakness. The boy with faith accomplished what the king with armor could not.

Theologically, the story teaches several truths. First, God uses weakness to shame strength. A shepherd boy with no armor defeated a warrior with unmatched power, demonstrating that salvation belongs to the Lord. This theme runs throughout Scripture, from barren Sarah giving birth to Gideon's three hundred men defeating a vast army, to the crucifixion of Christ, where apparent weakness became ultimate victory.

Second, faith sees differently. Where others calculated Goliath's size, David considered God's sufficiency. Faith does not deny reality but interprets it in light of God's promises.

Third, David's role points beyond himself to Christ. Just as David stood as Israel's representative, fighting on their behalf, so Christ stood as our representative, defeating sin and death at the cross. In both cases, God's anointed brought victory not by human means but by divine power.

Thus, 1 Samuel 17 is not a motivational tale about slaying personal giants. It is a gospel story, showing that God delivers his people through his chosen servant. David trusted the Lord when all others faltered, and God won the victory through him. This points forward to the greater David, Jesus Christ, who trusted his Father perfectly and won the decisive victory for his people. The story challenges us to stop relying on our own strength and to place our confidence fully in the God who saves.

APPLICATION

1. Faith sees what others miss

David saw Goliath not as an unbeatable giant but as an uncircumcised Philistine defying the living God. Faith looks at reality differently, interpreting challenges in light of God's promises rather than appearances. When others saw only danger, David saw covenant security. We, too, face giants—fear, doubt, temptation, suffering—that seem overwhelming. But faith fixes its eyes on God's power, not the size of the problem. This perspective changes everything. When we view life through the lens of God's faithfulness, giants shrink and God's sufficiency shines. Faith does not ignore obstacles; it sees them in the light of God's strength.

2. God's strength is revealed in weakness

The victory over Goliath was not about superior weapons but about God's power displayed through weakness. David's sling and stone looked foolish compared to Goliath's armor and spear, yet God chose the weak to shame the strong. This is the consistent rhythm of Scripture—God working through barren wombs, small armies, and a crucified Messiah. Our culture prizes strength, strategy, and resources, but God delights to show his power through unlikely vessels. When we feel inadequate, that is precisely when God can use us most powerfully. His strength is made perfect in weakness, and his glory shines brightest when our weakness yields to his might.

3. The battle belongs to the Lord

David's declaration to Goliath is a timeless truth: "The battle is the Lord's." We often live as if victory depends on our effort, strategy, or strength. But ultimate deliverance comes from God. This truth changes how we approach life's challenges. It frees us from paralyzing fear and from crushing pressure to control outcomes. When we face trials, we can trust that God is fighting for us. Our responsibility is not to muster heroic strength but to step forward in faith and obedience. The victory is his, not ours. And because he fights for us, we can live with courage, peace, and confidence in his promises.

4. Christ is the greater David

David's victory over Goliath points beyond itself to Christ's victory over sin and death. Just as David stood as Israel's representative, Christ stood in our place, defeating the enemy we could not conquer. David struck down the giant with a stone; Christ crushed the serpent by his cross and resurrection. The story of David and Goliath is not a motivational fable but a foreshadowing of the gospel. Our salvation does not rest in our courage but in Christ's triumph. He is the anointed King who wins the battle for his people. When we trust him, we share in his victory, secure in the power of the One who conquered the ultimate giant.

CONCLUSION

The story of David and Goliath is not about underdog heroics but about God's power to save through his anointed. David trusted the Lord when Saul and Israel trembled, and God delivered a stunning victory. This chapter teaches us that faith sees differently, that God's strength is revealed in weakness, and that the battle belongs to him. Ultimately, David's triumph points us to Christ, the greater David, who has defeated sin and death on our behalf. Our response is not to boast in ourselves but to trust fully in the God who saves through his chosen King.

REFLECTION

1. What made Goliath's challenge more than just a military threat?
2. How did David interpret Goliath differently than the rest of Israel?
3. Why did David refuse Saul's armor?
4. What was the theological point of David's speech to Goliath?
5. How does this story foreshadow Christ's victory for his people?

DISCUSSION

1. What "giants" in your life tempt you to focus on fear instead of faith?
2. How can faith change the way you see challenges?
3. Where do you feel weak, and how might God display his strength there?
4. What does it mean practically that the battle belongs to the Lord?
5. How does seeing Christ as the greater David shape your trust in him?

8

DAVID'S RISE, SAUL'S JEALOUSY

1 SAMUEL 18–20

Objective: To show that envy destroys, but covenant loyalty and God's providence preserve his anointed servant and people.

INTRODUCTION

After David's stunning victory over Goliath, his rise was meteoric. The people adored him, Jonathan loved him, and even Saul at first welcomed him. But admiration soon soured into jealousy. Saul's insecurity metastasized into paranoia, and the king who should have rejoiced in God's deliverer turned instead into his enemy. These chapters contrast Saul's envy with Jonathan's covenant loyalty, reminding us of both the danger of unchecked jealousy and the beauty of faithful friendship. Above all, we see God's hand preserving his chosen servant despite relentless opposition, pointing forward to the greater Son of David, whose life was likewise preserved from murderous schemes until his appointed hour.

EXAMINATION

Jonathan's covenant and Saul's jealousy (18:1–30)

The story continues with Jonathan's covenant with David. The son of Saul loved David as his own soul and sealed their friendship with a covenant. Jonathan even gave David his robe, armor, and weapons—symbols of his royal inheritance. In effect, Jonathan acknowledged David's future kingship. His humility and loyalty contrast sharply with Saul's insecurity. Saul initially kept David close, appointing him as a military commander. But as David succeeded, Saul's jealousy grew. The women's song, praising David above Saul, struck the king like a dagger: "Saul has slain his thousands, and David his tens of thousands." From that day forward, Saul viewed David with suspicion. Twice Saul hurled his spear at David, attempting to kill him. The refrain that "the Lord was with David, but had departed from Saul" captures the theological heart of the story.

Saul's schemes intensified. He offered David his daughter Merab, hoping David would die fighting the Philistines, but that plan failed. Then Saul gave Michal, who genuinely loved David, but again twisted the marriage into a plot for David's downfall. He demanded a bride price of one hundred Philistine foreskins, expecting David to perish in the attempt. Instead, David returned with two hundred, doubling the challenge and deepening Saul's fear. The irony is clear: every attempt to bring David down only elevated him further. God's favor ensured David's rise while Saul's decline became irreversible.

Saul's rage and God's preservation of David (19:1-24)

Saul's hostility became open. He ordered Jonathan and his servants to kill David. But Jonathan interceded, reminding Saul of David's loyalty and of the victory God had given through him. For a time, Saul relented, but soon jealousy overcame reason again. He attempted once more to pin David with his spear. David fled, and with Michal's help escaped Saul's assassins. Michal's deception with the household idol highlighted how divided Saul's own household had become. Even within his family, loyalty shifted toward David, exposing Saul's isolation. David sought refuge with Samuel at Ramah, but Saul's messengers—and even Saul himself—were overcome by the Spirit of God. Instead of seizing David, they prophesied, a striking picture of God's power frustrating human schemes.

Covenant loyalty and a tearful farewell (20:1-42)

This chapter centers on the covenant between David and Jonathan. Knowing Saul's hostility was growing, David sought Jonathan's help to discern the king's intentions. Jonathan devised a signal with arrows to warn David of danger. At a feast, Saul's rage boiled over when Jonathan defended David, and he even hurled a spear at his own son. This outburst showed how far envy had corrupted Saul, destroying not only his kingship but his family. Jonathan grieved deeply, but his loyalty to David never wavered. The chapter closes with their tearful farewell, as Jonathan reaffirmed that their covenant would extend to their descendants. It is one of Scripture's most moving portrayals of friendship, marked by sacrifice, faith, and loyalty.

Theologically, these chapters highlight several truths. First, envy is destructive. Saul's jealousy consumed him, corroded his character, and poisoned his relationships. What began as insecurity escalated into rage, deceit, and attempted murder. Envy blinded him to God's blessings and turned him against the very man who had delivered Israel.

Second, covenant loyalty is beautiful. Jonathan surrendered his own claim to the throne and risked his life to protect David. His humility and faith reflect God's own covenant love, steadfast and sacrificial.

Third, God's providence preserves his chosen servant. Despite Saul's relentless hostility, David was never harmed. God used Jonathan, Michal, and even the overpowering work of the Spirit to protect him.

Finally, these chapters point forward to Christ. Like David, Jesus was God's anointed, opposed by jealous leaders, yet preserved until his appointed hour. Jonathan's friendship anticipates the covenant loyalty of Christ, who lays down his life for his friends. Saul's jealousy warns us of the danger of resisting God's chosen King, while David's preservation reminds us of the invincibility of God's plan.

APPLICATION

1. Jealousy destroys relationships

Saul's jealousy of David consumed him. What began as insecurity grew into rage, deceit, and attempted murder. Jealousy corrodes the soul and poisons every relationship it touches. It blinds us to God's blessings and makes us view others as threats rather than gifts. When unchecked, envy leads to bitterness, resentment, and destructive behavior. We see this in Saul's life—his paranoia alienated him from David, Jonathan, Michal, and ultimately from God himself. The antidote to jealousy is gratitude. When we thank God for his blessings and trust his providence, we can rejoice in others' success instead of resenting it. Contentment frees us to love rather than compete.

2. God preserves his people

Despite Saul's relentless schemes, David was never harmed. Whether by Jonathan's intercession, Michal's deception, or the Spirit's overpowering work, God preserved his anointed. This is a reminder that God's purposes cannot be thwarted. Though enemies may rage and circumstances may seem dire, God guards his people. For believers, this truth is anchored in Christ. Just as David's life was preserved until God's appointed time, so Jesus' enemies could not touch him until his hour had come (see John 7:30; 8:30; 12:23). Likewise, our lives are in God's hands. Nothing can separate us from his love or derail his plans. This assurance gives us courage to trust him even in seasons of opposition and danger.

3. Covenant loyalty is costly but beautiful

Jonathan's friendship with David is one of the most remarkable relationships in Scripture. Though Jonathan was heir to the throne, he willingly acknowledged David as God's chosen king. He stripped himself of his royal robe and risked his life to protect his friend. True covenant loyalty is costly—it requires humility, sacrifice, and faith. But it is also beautiful, reflecting the steadfast love of God himself. Jonathan's example calls us to be faithful friends, spouses, and covenant partners, even when it costs us. In Christ, we experience the ultimate covenant loyalty. He gave up his glory, laid down his life, and calls us to embody that same faithful love in our relationships.

4. Christ is the greater David

David's rise and Saul's hostility foreshadow the life of Christ. Like David, Jesus was God's anointed, hated without cause, and plotted against by jealous leaders. Yet God preserved him until the appointed time, and through his death and resurrection, secured deliverance for his people. Saul's envy warns us of rejecting God's chosen King, while Jonathan's loyalty points us to the joy of trusting him. Christ is the friend who sticks closer than a brother (Prov. 18:24), the King who reigns in faithfulness, and the Savior who secures our covenant with God. When we face hostility or rejection, we can take heart that we belong to the King who triumphed over every enemy and will preserve us to the end.

CONCLUSION

In 1 Samuel 18–20, Saul's jealousy spiraled into rage, but God's providence preserved David. Jonathan's covenant loyalty stands as a shining contrast to Saul's envy, reminding us of the beauty of faithfulness and the danger of jealousy. These chapters point us ultimately to Christ, the greater David, who was preserved until his hour came and who now reigns as King. Our response is to reject jealousy, embrace covenant loyalty, and trust the God who preserves his people through every trial.

REFLECTION

1. How did Jonathan demonstrate covenant loyalty to David?
2. What role did Saul's jealousy play in his downfall?
3. How did God preserve David from Saul's schemes?
4. What does Jonathan's example teach us about friendship and faithfulness?
5. How do these chapters foreshadow Christ's experience of opposition?

DISCUSSION

1. Where do you struggle with jealousy, and how can gratitude overcome it?
2. How have you seen God preserve you through difficult seasons?
3. What does covenant loyalty look like in your closest relationships?
4. How does Jonathan's humility challenge you to put others above yourself?
5. What encouragement do you draw from seeing Christ as the greater David?

9

DAVID ON THE RUN
1 SAMUEL 21–23

Objective: To show that even when fear drives failure, God's providence and grace preserve his chosen servant.

INTRODUCTION

These chapters depict David at one of the most vulnerable points in his life. Hunted by Saul, he fled from place to place, often acting in fear rather than faith. He lied to Ahimelech, feigned madness before Achish, and barely escaped multiple attempts on his life. Yet even in his panic, God preserved him, using unexpected people and places to protect his anointed. By chapter 23, David began to recover his faith, seeking God's guidance and depending once more on his word. These stories remind us that even God's chosen servants stumble, but his grace and providence never fail.

EXAMINATION

The story of David in 1 Samuel 21–23 offers one of the most vivid portraits of God's anointed living as a fugitive. Though destined for the throne, David spent years fleeing for his life, caught between panic and prayer. These chapters reveal both his weakness and God's preserving grace, reminding us that God's purposes are never thwarted, even when his servants stumble.

Fear and failure at Nob and Gath (21:1-15)

The chapter begins with David's flight to Nob, where he met Ahimelech the priest. Afraid to tell the truth, David lied, claiming he was on a mission for Saul. Ahimelech, unsuspecting, gave him the consecrated bread and the sword of Goliath. While David's deceit would later bring tragedy, God's providence was evident. The bread symbolized God's provision for his servant, and the sword recalled God's past deliverance. Yet the presence of Doeg the Edomite foreshadowed calamity, for he would later report to Saul.

From Nob, David fled to Gath, seeking protection among the Philistines—the very enemies he had once defeated. Recognized as Israel's champion, he panicked and pretended to be insane, scratching at doors and drooling down his beard. The ruse worked, and Achish dismissed him as harmless. This episode shows David at his lowest: fearful, faithless, and undignified. Yet God preserved him, turning even humiliation into deliverance. Psalms 34 and 56, composed from this experience, reveal how David later acknowledged God's hand in rescuing him when he had no strength of his own.

Refuge and tragedy at Adullam and Nob (22:1-23)

This chapter shifts the focus to David's gathering followers. In the cave of Adullam, he was joined by about four hundred men described as distressed, indebted, or bitter in soul. This unlikely company became the foundation of his kingdom, a reminder that God builds with the weak and broken rather than the powerful. David also sought safety for his parents in Moab, but the prophet Gad directed him to remain in Judah, underscoring that God's purposes would unfold in the land of promise. Even in exile, David could not escape God's calling.

Meanwhile, Saul descended further into paranoia. When he heard that David had visited Nob, he accused the priests of conspiracy. Ahimelech defended his innocence, but Saul ordered their death. His guards refused, but Doeg the Edomite slaughtered eighty-five priests and destroyed the city. This massacre epitomized Saul's corruption: the king tasked with protecting God's people turned against them. Abiathar, the lone survivor, fled to David with the ephod, giving David the ability to inquire of the Lord. In the ashes of Nob's destruction, God provided his anointed with a new means of guidance.

Guidance and deliverance at Keilah and Maon (23:1–29)

In chapter 23, David began to recover his faith. When the Philistines attacked Keilah, David twice inquired of the Lord before acting. God promised victory, and though his men feared, David obeyed and delivered the city. But when Saul plotted to trap him there, David again sought God's guidance and escaped. The ephod became a tangible reminder that true strength lies not in human cleverness but in seeking God's will. This marked a shift from panic to prayer, from fear to faith.

The chapter also highlights Jonathan's loyalty. Jonathan sought out David at Horesh and "strengthened his hand in God," reminding him of God's promises and affirming their covenant. Though heir to the throne, Jonathan acknowledged that David would be king. His encouragement provided David with hope in a season of despair. Jonathan's covenant faithfulness shines against Saul's treachery, showing the beauty of loyal friendship rooted in God's promises.

Saul's pursuit intensified, and at Maon he nearly trapped David. But just as Saul closed in, news of a Philistine raid forced him to withdraw. The place was called the Rock of Escape, a lasting testimony to God's providential timing. The narrative reminds us that God's deliverance comes not a moment too soon or too late. David was preserved, not because of his cunning, but because God's purposes could not fail.

Theologically, these chapters teach several lessons. First, fear often leads to failure. David's lies and feigned madness show how panic can cloud judgment and drive us to compromise.

Second, God's providence preserves his people despite their failures. Bread, sword, cave, ephod, covenant friend, and even enemy raids were all means of God's protection.

Third, prayer is the turning point. When David sought God's guidance, he found stability again.

Finally, these events foreshadow Christ. Like David, Jesus was pursued by enemies, betrayed, and surrounded by the weak and broken. But unlike David, he never faltered in faith. In Christ, we see the perfect trust that secures salvation for his people, and we find assurance that God's purposes will prevail even when we stumble.

APPLICATION

1. Fear leads to failure

David's panic at Nob and Gath shows how fear can push us into rash and sinful choices. Fear magnifies problems and shrinks faith, tempting us to lie, compromise, or run instead of trusting God. Yet even in failure, God's grace meets us. The gospel does not excuse fear, but it assures us that our weakness does not cancel God's faithfulness. When fear tempts us to act foolishly, we must remember that God's promises are stronger than our panic. He is faithful even when we falter, and his grace can redeem even our missteps for his purposes.

2. God preserves his people through providence

Throughout these chapters, God preserved David in remarkable ways—through consecrated bread, a sword, a cave, friends, and even enemy raids. Providence means that God quietly but powerfully orders events for his people's good. We may not always see his hand, but it is always at work. This truth brings comfort in trials: our survival does not rest on our cleverness but on God's care. Nothing can thwart his purposes or snatch us from his hand (John 10:28). Just as David was preserved for kingship, so God preserves us for his kingdom, guarding us until the day of Christ Jesus.

3. Prayer turns panic into peace

The turning point in these chapters comes when David inquired of the Lord. When he sought God's counsel at Keilah and Ziph, he found direction and deliverance. Prayer transforms panic into peace because it reorients us to God's sovereignty. Instead of reacting in fear, we can respond in faith. In seasons of uncertainty, our first instinct should be to seek God's word and will. Like David with the ephod, we now have access through Christ our High Priest. When we bring our fears to him, he gives wisdom, courage, and calm. Prayer doesn't remove problems, but it gives us peace to walk through them with God's presence.

4. Christ is our Rock of Escape

The Rock of Escape in chapter 23 reminds us that God delivers his people at just the right time. For David, it was rescue from Saul's army. For us, it is deliverance through Christ. Jesus is our ultimate refuge, the Rock who saves us not only from earthly enemies but from sin and death. Like David, we are pursued by dangers too great for us. But Christ has already won the victory, and in him we are safe. When fear surrounds us, we run not to caves or schemes but to Christ, our refuge and fortress. In him, we find the security and salvation no enemy can take away.

CONCLUSION

In 1 Samuel 21–23, David fled in fear, stumbled in faith, and yet was preserved by God's providence. These chapters show us the danger of fear, the beauty of prayer, and the assurance of God's preserving grace. Though David faltered, God's plan never did. His servant was kept safe until the day he would reign. Ultimately, these events point us to Christ, our greater David, who trusted perfectly and delivers completely. Our call is to seek God in prayer, trust his providence, and rest in his preserving hand.

REFLECTION

1. Why did David lie to Ahimelech at Nob, and what were the consequences?
2. How did God preserve David even in his panic at Gath?
3. What kind of men gathered to David at Adullam, and why is this significant?
4. How did Abiathar's arrival with the ephod change David's ability to seek God?
5. What was the Rock of Escape, and what does it teach us about God's providence?

DISCUSSION

1. When have you been tempted to let fear drive your decisions?
2. How have you experienced God's providence preserving you in hard times?
3. What does it look like for you to turn panic into prayer today?
4. How does Jonathan's encouragement strengthen your picture of Christian friendship?
5. In what ways is Christ your Rock of Escape in life's battles?

10

SPARING THE LORD'S ANOINTED

1 SAMUEL 24, 26

Objective: To show that true faith waits on God's timing, choosing mercy and integrity over power and impatience.

INTRODUCTION

When Saul stumbled into a cave at En-gedi and later lay asleep in the wilderness of Ziph, David had the perfect opportunity to end his fugitive life. One thrust of a sword, and the crown would be his. David's men urged him to act, quoting what seemed like divine confirmation: "Here is the day of which the Lord said to you." From a nearsighted perspective, the choice was obvious—take the shortcut, grasp the crown, stop the madness. But David saw what others did not. He looked beyond the immediate to God's larger promise. Twice he refused to lay a hand on the Lord's anointed, showing that faith waits on God rather than seizing power prematurely.

EXAMINATION

The story of David sparing Saul in 1 Samuel 24 and 26 offers some of the clearest insight into David's heart and his theology of kingship. In both episodes, David faced the same temptation: seize the throne by shedding Saul's blood. His men urged him on, appealing even to divine providence. But David resisted, choosing patience over expedience, mercy over violence, and trust over self-assertion. The repetition of these two stories underscores their importance: the narrator wants us to slow down, compare the details, and see how David's restraint defined his rise as God's chosen king.

Mercy in the cave at En-gedi (24:1–22)

This chapter begins with Saul's pursuit of David in the wilderness of En-gedi. With three thousand soldiers, Saul vastly outnumbered David's small band. By providence, Saul entered a cave to relieve himself—the very cave where David and his men were hiding. David's men whispered that this was the moment, interpreting coincidence as confirmation: surely God had delivered Saul into David's hand. The language of "hand" dominates these chapters, emphasizing who truly controls the outcome. At first, David crept forward and cut off a corner of Saul's robe. But his conscience bothered him. The robe symbolized Saul's kingship, and cutting it was an act of symbolic rebellion. David immediately regretted even this gesture and rebuked his men, insisting that he would not lift his hand against the Lord's anointed.

When Saul left the cave, David followed him out, bowing low and addressing him respectfully as "my lord the king" and "my father." He presented the corner of the robe as evidence of his innocence: he could have killed Saul but chose not to. David contrasted Saul's pursuit of his life with his own refusal to harm Saul, arguing that wicked men act wickedly but he would entrust his case to the Lord, the righteous judge. His self-description as a dead dog or a flea highlighted his humility: he posed no real threat to Saul's throne. Twice he appealed to God to adjudicate between them. David would not grasp the crown like Adam grasped the fruit; he would wait for God to give it.

Saul's response was emotional but shallow. He wept, acknowledged David's righteousness, and admitted that David would one day be king. He even asked David to spare his descendants, to which David swore an oath. Yet the repentance was short-lived. Saul soon resumed his pursuit. His words, though tearful, revealed a pattern of recycled repentance—confession without transformation.

Restraint in the wilderness of Ziph (26:1–25)

This story repeats the test, this time in the wilderness of Ziph. Again the Ziphites betrayed David's location. Saul marched with three thousand men. David scouted the camp and found Saul asleep, his spear—the emblem of his violent reign—stuck in the ground by his head. Abishai, David's fiery nephew, urged him to strike: "Let me pin him to the earth with one stroke of the spear." To Abishai, this was providence. To David, it was temptation. He refused, declaring, "Who can put out his hand against the Lord's anointed and be guiltless?" Instead, David outlined three ways Saul might fall—by divine judgment, natural death, or battle—but in none of them would David seize power illegitimately. Taking Saul's life would corrupt his kingship before it began. Power gained by violence breeds violence. David chose to trust God's promise instead.

David and Abishai took Saul's spear and water jar, symbols of power and life. Back on a hillside, David mocked Abner for failing to guard the king and displayed the stolen items as proof. He again appealed to God as judge, insisting that his restraint proved his faithfulness. Saul responded once more with confession, admitting sin and blessing David. But as before, his words were hollow. David placed no trust in Saul's promises; his hope was in God's justice. "The Lord rewards every man for his righteousness and faithfulness," David declared, entrusting his future to God's hand.

Theologically, these chapters emphasize three lessons. First, power: Saul embodied violent, insecure power, but David revealed true strength through restraint and mercy.

Second, perspective: David's men saw opportunity; David saw temptation. Faith interprets circumstances not by immediacy but by God's promises.

Third, promise: David trusted that God would deliver the kingdom in his time. He refused shortcuts, knowing that crowns seized in haste become curses. The repetition of these two stories reinforces the point: David's rise would be marked not by bloodshed but by faith.

Ultimately, these chapters point beyond David to Christ. Like David, Jesus faced the temptation to seize power prematurely—Satan offered him the kingdoms of the world without the cross. But Jesus refused, choosing trust and obedience. Like David, he spared his enemies, praying from the cross, "Father, forgive them." Where Saul's spear symbolized violence, the cross symbolizes mercy. David's restraint foreshadows the mercy of the greater Son of David, who won the kingdom not by the sword but by sacrifice. In him, we see the fullness of power, perspective, and promise.

APPLICATION

1. Don't grasp what God has promised

David twice refused to seize the throne by killing Saul, even when the opportunity seemed providential. He trusted God's timing and would not shortcut God's plan. We face similar temptations to grasp for control—to manipulate outcomes in relationships, careers, or ministry. But shortcuts reveal unbelief. Faith waits. Faith resists the lure of expediency and entrusts the future to God. Waiting is hard, but crowns seized in haste become burdens. David shows us that real trust means refusing to take by force what God has promised to give in his time.

2. Symbols are not substitutes

Saul's spear and water jar represented his authority and survival, yet neither could save him. We also rely on props—money, possessions, status, achievements—but they are as fragile as Saul's spear when God is absent. The story reminds us that symbols cannot replace substance. True security lies not in what we hold but in who holds us. When God is with us, we are safe regardless of appearances. When God departs, no symbol, title, or resource can preserve us. Faith clings not to symbols but to the living God, who alone sustains and delivers.

3. Beware of recycled repentance

Twice Saul confessed, even weeping, but his repentance proved shallow. Words without change are noise. We too can fall into patterns of recycled repentance—saying the right things, feeling the right emotions, but never turning from sin. God calls us to genuine contrition, repentance that bears fruit. Confession is the beginning, not the end. True repentance changes direction, seeks accountability, and pursues holiness. Saul's hollow remorse warns us not to mistake feelings for faith. God desires truth in the inward being, not rehearsed words or temporary sorrow. Real repentance is transformation, not repetition.

4. See enemies through God's perspective

David consistently referred to Saul as the Lord's anointed, even while Saul sought his life. David's perspective restrained vengeance and preserved his integrity. We live in a culture that justifies retaliation, but God calls us to see others—even enemies—through his perspective. Every person bears his image. Every rival is someone God may yet redeem. When we adopt this perspective, it reshapes our speech, tempers our anger, and cultivates mercy. To see enemies through God's eyes is to reflect the mercy of Christ, who loved us when we were his enemies and gave his life to reconcile us to God.

CONCLUSION

In 1 Samuel 24 and 26, David twice resisted the temptation to seize power by killing Saul. He entrusted himself to God's justice and timing, showing that true power is found in patience and mercy. Saul's shallow repentance contrasts with David's farsighted restraint. Ultimately, these stories point to Christ, the greater Son of David, who refused shortcuts, trusted his Father, and showed mercy to his enemies. Our call is to reject shortcuts, embrace integrity, and trust the God who keeps his promises in his time and way.

REFLECTION

1. Why did David regret cutting Saul's robe in chapter 24?
2. How did David argue for his innocence before Saul?
3. What did Saul's spear symbolize in chapter 26?
4. Why did David refuse to kill Saul, even when urged by his men?
5. How do these episodes highlight God's providence and David's faith?

DISCUSSION

1. What shortcuts tempt you to grasp control instead of trusting God?
2. How do we sometimes rely on symbols instead of God?
3. What does real repentance look like compared to Saul's recycled remorse?
4. How can seeing others as God's image-bearers restrain vengeance?
5. In what ways does Christ fulfill David's picture of mercy and restraint?

11

ABIGAIL'S WISE INTERVENTION
1 SAMUEL 25

Objective: To show that God restrains anger and accomplishes justice through wise intercession, preserving his servants by grace.

INTRODUCTION

In 1 Samuel 25, David faced a very similar test to the one in chapters 24 and 26. There, he resisted killing Saul, entrusting judgment to God. Here, provoked by Nabal's insult, David nearly gave in to rage. The man after God's heart strapped on his sword and prepared to slaughter an entire household. But God, in mercy, sent Abigail, a woman of wisdom and courage, to intercede. Her discernment preserved her family, restrained David from bloodguilt, and pointed to God's justice. This chapter reminds us that folly destroys, wisdom saves, and God's providence works through unlikely instruments to keep his servant on course.

EXAMINATION

Nabal's folly and David's anger (25:1-13)

The chapter begins with Samuel's death, a significant loss for Israel. The nation mourned the prophet who had guided them, and David himself lost a key spiritual anchor. Into this moment of grief and instability comes the story of Nabal and Abigail, showing how David would be tested not only in battle but also in his personal integrity.

David had been protecting the shepherds of Nabal, a wealthy Calebite with thousands of sheep and goats. Shearing time was a season of celebration, generosity, and feasting, when landowners customarily rewarded those who had shown loyalty. David sent messengers politely requesting provisions, reminding Nabal of the protection his men had received. Nabal's response, however, was contemptuous. He sneered, "Who is David? Who is the son of Jesse?" By dismissing David as a runaway servant, Nabal not only insulted him personally but also rejected the Lord's anointed. The text underscores his character: harsh, surly, and foolish. His arrogance put his entire household at risk.

David's reaction was swift and alarming. In chapter 24, he had spared Saul, trusting God to act. But here, wounded pride clouded his judgment. He told his men to strap on their swords, and four hundred warriors marched toward Nabal's house. David's words reveal his intent: "God do so to David and more also, if by morning I leave so much as one male of all who belong to him." This was not measured justice but vengeful rage. The narrator highlights the contrast: David, who had resisted killing Israel's king, was ready to annihilate a household over an insult. Even a man after God's heart was vulnerable to anger and folly.

Abigail's wisdom and intercession (25:14–31)

Enter Abigail, Nabal's wife, described as intelligent and beautiful. When a servant warned her of the danger, she acted decisively. She quickly prepared a generous gift of bread, wine, meat, and grain and rode out to intercept David. Her approach was marked by humility: she bowed before David, took guilt upon herself, and pleaded for mercy. Her speech is one of the longest given by a woman in Scripture and rich with theology. She urged David not to stain his conscience with bloodguilt or take vengeance with his own hand. She reminded him that the Lord would establish his house and fight his battles. She appealed to God's promises, pointing David to his future kingship. By lifting his eyes from the heat of anger to the hope of God's covenant, Abigail redirected his path.

David's response shows how powerful her words were. He blessed the Lord for sending her, blessed her discernment, and blessed her for restraining him from sin. He admitted that without her intervention, he would have destroyed every male in Nabal's household. Abigail became the human instrument of God's providence, saving David from an act that would have haunted his conscience and damaged his claim to the throne.

God's justice and David's vindication (25:32–44)

The story then turns to God's judgment. When Abigail told Nabal what had nearly happened, his heart failed him, and he became like a stone. Ten days later, the Lord struck him, and he died. The timing underscores that vengeance belongs to God, not to David. Where David nearly acted in anger, God acted in justice. David praised the Lord for vindicating him without his own hand being stained with blood. God himself removed the fool who had insulted his anointed, demonstrating that divine justice is always better than human vengeance.

The chapter concludes with David sending for Abigail, who became his wife. Her wisdom, courage, and humility made her a fitting partner for Israel's future king. In contrast to Nabal's arrogance, Abigail embodied godly discernment and peacemaking. Her story illustrates the truth that wisdom preserves life and aligns itself with God's purposes.

Theologically, several themes emerge. First, pride and folly lead to ruin. Nabal's arrogance endangered his household and brought about his death.

Second, unchecked anger endangers even the faithful. David's near failure reminds us of our need to guard our hearts.

Third, God provides intercessors. Abigail stood in the gap, foreshadowing Christ, who bore guilt not his own and turned away wrath.

Fourth, God vindicates his servants. David was spared from sin, and justice was carried out in God's way and time. This chapter reminds us that God's people are preserved not by their perfection but by his providence and grace.

APPLICATION

1. Guard your heart against rash anger

David nearly committed mass slaughter because of wounded pride. Anger magnifies insults, distorts judgment, and drives us to sin. Scripture warns that human anger does not produce God's righteousness. Like David, we are vulnerable to lashing out when dishonored. The lesson is clear: anger may flare quickly, but we must pause, pray, and entrust the situation to God. Left unchecked, rage can ruin reputations, relationships, and integrity. God calls us to slow down our reactions, seeking his wisdom rather than feeding our fury. Righteousness is not achieved through rage but through trust in God's justice.

2. Value the wisdom of peacemakers

Abigail's discernment preserved lives and redirected David's path. She spoke truth with humility, courage, and urgency. God often places peacemakers in our lives to calm conflict and remind us of his promises. The challenge is whether we will listen. Peacemaking is not weakness but strength—it takes courage to step into tension with grace and truth. In families, churches, and communities, God calls us to be like Abigail, interceding, speaking wisdom, and pursuing peace. Blessed are the peacemakers, Jesus said, for they reflect the character of their Father in heaven.

3. Trust God to vindicate you

David was spared from bloodguilt because Abigail intervened and because God acted in justice. Nabal's death came not from David's sword but from the Lord's hand. This underscores a vital truth: vengeance belongs to God. When wronged, we are tempted to retaliate, to take matters into our own hands. But God calls us to release the outcome to him. He alone judges perfectly, and his timing is flawless. When we trust God to vindicate us, we are freed from bitterness and rage. Faith waits for God to act, knowing his justice is always better than our revenge.

4. Abigail as a type of Christ

Abigail stepped between David's wrath and Nabal's folly, taking guilt upon herself and pleading for mercy. This anticipates Christ, who interceded for us by bearing our guilt and turning away God's wrath. Her humility, courage, and wisdom foreshadow the greater Intercessor, who not only prevented bloodshed but secured eternal salvation. Just as David blessed Abigail for keeping him from sin, we bless Christ who saves us from destruction. Her story reminds us of the gospel truth: we are spared because another stood in the gap. In Christ, God provides the perfect mediator who reconciles us to himself.

CONCLUSION

Firsat Samuel 25 presents a vivid contrast: Nabal's folly, David's anger, and Abigail's wisdom. Through her intervention, God preserved David from sin and brought justice on Nabal. This story reminds us that folly destroys, anger endangers, and wisdom preserves. Above all, it points us to Christ, the true Intercessor who stands between wrath and destruction. Our response is to guard against anger, listen to wise counsel, trust God's justice, and rejoice in the One who intercedes for us with perfect mercy and grace.

REFLECTION

1. Why was Nabal's insult so significant?
2. How did David's reaction here differ from his restraint with Saul?
3. What was remarkable about Abigail's speech to David?
4. How did God vindicate David without his sword?
5. What theological lessons emerge from this story?

DISCUSSION

1. When have you been tempted to act rashly in anger?
2. Who has been an Abigail in your life, speaking wisdom in conflict?
3. How can we practice waiting for God's justice instead of seeking revenge?
4. What does it mean for us to be peacemakers in today's world?
5. How does Abigail's intercession point us to Christ's greater work of salvation?

12

DAVID AMONG THE PHILISTINES
1 SAMUEL 27, 29–30

Objective: To show that despair and compromise cannot derail God's providence, who restores and strengthens his people.

INTRODUCTION

After years of being pursued by Saul, David reached a breaking point. Convinced that survival was impossible in Israel, he fled to the Philistines. What began as a strategy for safety led to compromise and deception. Yet even in this season of doubt, God preserved him from greater sin and restored him after disaster. These chapters reveal both David's weakness and God's faithfulness. They remind us that while God's people stumble, his purposes never fail. In Ziklag's ashes, David learned again to find strength in the Lord, a lesson as relevant for us today as it was for him.

EXAMINATION

The narrative of 1 Samuel 27, 29, and 30 presents David in a season of deep weakness but also of remarkable restoration. After years of fleeing Saul, David finally gave in to despair. Convinced that Saul would never stop pursuing him, he reasoned that his only hope was to seek refuge among Israel's enemies. It was a striking lapse of faith. The one who had once proclaimed that the Lord delivers from sword and spear now sought safety in Philistine territory. Compromise seemed easier than trust.

Despair and compromise in Philistia (27:1-12)

In chapter 27, David entered Gath under the protection of Achish and was granted Ziklag as his base. From there, David conducted raids on Amalekites and other desert tribes, but he lied to Achish, claiming he had attacked Israelite allies. His strategy bought him time and security, but at the cost of deception and moral compromise. Instead of openly trusting God, David relied on manipulation to survive. The narrator gives no evidence of David seeking the Lord in this period, underscoring his spiritual dryness. David's choice warns us how despair can lead to compromise when faith grows dim.

Providence and prevention through the Philistines (29:1-11)

By chapter 29, this compromise nearly resulted in catastrophe. As the Philistines assembled to fight Israel, Achish insisted that David and his men would join him. The thought of God's anointed king fighting against God's people is unthinkable, yet this is where fear had led him. Only the suspicion of the Philistine commanders spared David. They demanded that Achish send him home, fearing he might turn traitor in battle. Ironically, it was pagan generals who preserved David from betraying his calling. God's providence intervened to keep his servant from a disastrous choice. Even when David was faithless, God remained faithful.

Restoration and renewal (30:1-31)

This chapter recounts the lowest point of David's journey. While he and his men were away, the Amalekites raided Ziklag, burning the city and carrying off wives, children, and possessions. Returning to ruins, David and his men wept until they had no strength left. Grief turned to bitterness, and the people spoke of stoning him. David had lost everything—family, home, and the loyalty of his men. It was a moment of complete despair. Yet in this dark hour comes a turning point: "But David strengthened himself in the Lord his God." This brief sentence marks a shift from fear to faith. For the first time in this narrative, David turned back to God. He sought the Lord's counsel through Abiathar the priest and received a clear promise: "Pursue, for you shall surely overtake and shall surely rescue."

With renewed strength, David set out in pursuit. Along the way, two hundred men were too exhausted to continue, leaving only four hundred to press on. Yet even this weakness was part of God's providence. An abandoned Egyptian slave, left to die by the Amalekites, became the key to finding their camp. What looked like a liability became an instrument of victory. David attacked, defeated the Amalekites, and recovered everything. The text stresses the completeness of restoration: "Nothing was missing, whether small or great, sons or daughters, spoil or anything that had been taken. David brought back all." In place of ashes and despair came triumph and restoration.

A new test arose after the victory. Some of David's men wanted to withhold the spoil from those who had stayed behind at the brook Besor. David, however, insisted that all should share alike. The victory was the Lord's gift, not theirs to hoard. His fairness not only preserved unity but also established a lasting statute in Israel. The man who had once faltered in fear was restored as a leader marked by generosity and trust in God's grace. True kingship is measured not by seizing but by sharing, not by self-interest but by selflessness.

Theologically, these chapters offer several lessons. First, despair can erode faith and lead to compromise, as seen in David's flight to Philistia.

Second, God's providence is sovereign even in our failures. He preserved David from fighting Israel through the objections of Philistine commanders.

Third, God restores his people when they turn back to him. At Ziklag, David's despair gave way to renewed strength when he sought the Lord.

Fourth, God's deliverance is complete—nothing was lost in the Amalekite raid, reminding us that his restoration goes beyond survival to fullness.

Fifth, restored faith expresses itself in generosity. David's decision to share spoil reflected God's own gracious character.

Ultimately, these chapters point us to Christ. Like David, Jesus was rejected and lived as a sojourner. But unlike David, he never faltered in faith. At the cross, ruin seemed total, yet God brought complete victory through his resurrection. Where David strengthened himself in the Lord to recover what was lost, Christ triumphed over sin and death to secure eternal restoration for his people. In him we find the greater King who turns despair into hope and ashes into joy. David stumbled, but Christ never did. Our security rests not in our strength but in his faithfulness, which restores fully and forever.

APPLICATION

1. Fear leads to compromise

David fled to Philistia out of despair, convinced Saul would destroy him. Fear drove him to seek safety outside God's promises. We too are tempted to compromise when fear grips us—choosing security, approval, or shortcuts rather than trusting God. Fear magnifies threats and shrinks faith, leading us away from obedience. David's example warns us that compromise never brings true peace. The antidote is to strengthen ourselves in the Lord, remembering his promises. Faith does not deny danger but trusts God above it. Only when our hope rests in him are we free to live faithfully without compromise.

2. God's providence overrules our failures

David's compromise placed him on the brink of disaster, but God intervened through Philistine commanders who rejected him. Even when David's faith faltered, God's purposes held firm. This is good news for us. Our failures are real, but they do not derail God's plan. Providence means that God weaves even our missteps into his larger design. Instead of despairing over past mistakes, we can trust his ability to redeem them. Like David, we may find that God's hand has preserved us from greater ruin than we imagined. His purposes are unshakable, even when our faith wavers.

3. Find strength in the Lord

At Ziklag, when everything seemed lost, David turned to the Lord and was renewed. This was the hinge of the story. Strength is not found in resources, strategies, or even loyal supporters, but in God alone. We face moments of despair when losses overwhelm us and people fail us. In those moments, the call is to do what David did: seek God, pour out our hearts, and find strength in his presence. Prayer, Scripture, and worship lift our eyes from ruins to the Redeemer. When we strengthen ourselves in the Lord, despair gives way to hope, and weakness becomes courage.

4. God restores fully

The Amalekites left Ziklag in ashes, and David's men thought all was lost. Yet

God promised, "You shall surely rescue," and he fulfilled it completely. Not a single person was missing. God's deliverance is not partial but total. This points us to the gospel, where Christ restores more than what sin has ruined. He does not merely salvage fragments; he makes all things new. When we despair that too much has been lost—time, relationships, opportunities—we remember Ziklag. God restores fully in his time. The ashes of defeat can become the place where God reveals his power to redeem and renew.

CONCLUSION

First Samuel 27, 29–30 shows David at his weakest and strongest. Fear led him to compromise, yet God's providence preserved him. Despair at Ziklag turned into renewal when he strengthened himself in the Lord. God's deliverance restored everything that seemed lost, and David's leadership reflected generosity and faith. These chapters remind us that though we stumble, God remains faithful. Ultimately, they point to Christ, who never wavered and whose victory secures complete restoration. Our call is to trust his providence, seek his strength, and rest in his power to redeem.

REFLECTION

1. Why did David flee to Philistine territory, and what does it reveal about his faith?
2. How did God's providence prevent David from fighting against Israel?
3. What was the significance of David strengthening himself in the Lord?
4. How did God demonstrate complete restoration at Ziklag?
5. How do these chapters foreshadow Christ's greater victory?

DISCUSSION

1. What compromises are you tempted to make when fear overwhelms you?
2. How have you seen God's providence redeem your failures?
3. What does it mean for you to strengthen yourself in the Lord?
4. Where do you need to trust God for restoration in your life?
5. How does Christ's complete victory give you hope in times of despair?

13

SAUL'S FINAL NIGHT & DEATH

1 SAMUEL 28, 31

Objective: To show that Saul's downfall warns against rebellion and despair while pointing to Christ, the faithful King.

INTRODUCTION

The story of Saul ends in tragedy. Once chosen by God and filled with the Spirit, Saul descended into fear, jealousy, and rebellion. In his final hours, cut off from divine guidance, he sought counsel from a forbidden source. At En-dor, he turned to a medium, sealing his rejection of God. Soon after, on the slopes of Mount Gilboa, he fell before the Philistines, his death marking the end of a failed kingship. These chapters serve as a sobering warning: to turn from God is to walk the path of despair. Yet they also highlight God's faithfulness to his word and the contrast between Saul and David, pointing us ultimately to Christ, the true King.

EXAMINATION

God's silence and Saul's desperation (28:1–25)

This story unfolds against the backdrop of looming war. The Philistines gathered at Shunem, while Israel camped across the valley. Saul trembled when he saw the enemy's vast army. He inquired of the Lord, but God gave no answer—no dreams, no prophets, no Urim. This silence was judgment, the result of years of disobedience. Saul had ignored God's commands, rejected Samuel's rebukes, and pursued his own will. Now he reaped the fruit of his rebellion. Silence from God is not indifference but the terrifying consequence of hardened sin.

Desperate, Saul turned to what he had once outlawed. He disguised himself and sought a medium (not a witch) at En-dor. The irony is stark: the king who had purged the land of necromancers now relied on one. This act represented ultimate rebellion—seeking guidance apart from God. Though he longed for answers, he still refused repentance. The medium attempted her craft, but when Samuel actually appeared, she cried out in fear. This was no illusion. God himself permitted Samuel to confront Saul with a final word of judgment.

Samuel's message was blunt: the kingdom had been torn from Saul and given to David. The Lord had turned against him because of his disobedience. Defeat was certain. By the next day, Saul and his sons would fall. This was not new information but the confirmation of what Saul had long resisted. The scene ends with Saul collapsed in fear, eating a last meal prepared by the medium. The once tall and proud king was reduced to a trembling figure awaiting death.

The fall of Saul and the fulfillment of judgment (31:1-13)

The final chapter of 1 Samuel records the fulfillment of Samuel's prophecy. The Philistines struck Israel on Mount Gilboa. Saul's sons fell first, including Jonathan, whose covenant loyalty to David had shone brightly amid Saul's darkness. With his heirs dead and the enemy pressing close, Saul was struck by archers. Unwilling to be captured and tortured, he fell on his own sword. His armor-bearer followed, and Israel's army fled. The Philistines desecrated Saul's body, fastening it to the wall of Beth-shan. Only the men of Jabesh-gilead, grateful for Saul's earlier rescue of their city, showed honor by retrieving and burying the bodies. Thus, the narrator chooses not to "preach Saul into hell" but to recall his finest hour.

But the Chronicler underscores the theological meaning of Saul's death. "So Saul died for his breach of faith. He broke faith with the Lord in that he did not keep the command of the Lord, and also consulted a medium, seeking guidance. He did not seek guidance from the Lord. Therefore the Lord put him to death and turned the kingdom over to David" (1 Chron. 10:13–14). Saul's end was not mere tragedy but divine judgment. His reign began with promise but ended in despair because he refused to obey God.

Placed alongside David's story, the contrast is striking. While Saul grasped at forbidden counsel, David sought the Lord at Ziklag and found restoration. While Saul fell on Gilboa, David was preserved and strengthened. Two kings faced crisis—one turned from God and died, the other turned to God and lived. The stories teach us that life is found not in self-reliance but in humble dependence on the Lord.

Several theological truths emerge. First, persistent disobedience leads to God's silence and judgment. Saul's refusal to repent hardened into despair.

Second, forbidden substitutes never provide true guidance. Saul's séance produced not hope but doom.

Third, God's word always comes to pass. Samuel's earlier rebukes found fulfillment in Saul's death.

Fourth, leadership without faith brings ruin, not only for Saul but for his sons and people.

Finally, the contrast with David points beyond both men to Christ. Saul failed utterly, David faltered often, but Christ never failed. Where Saul fell on Gilboa, Christ triumphed at Calvary. Where Saul's death brought defeat, Christ's death brought victory. The end of Saul's story highlights our desperate need for a perfect King, one who obeys fully and reigns forever—the One who died yet is now alive forevermore (Rev. 1:18).

APPLICATION

1. Silence from God is serious

When Saul inquired of the Lord and received no answer, it was not neglect but judgment. Years of disobedience had hardened him, and God allowed him to feel the full weight of rejection. This reminds us never to take lightly the voice of God. When he speaks through Scripture, conscience, or wise counsel, we must listen. To ignore his Word repeatedly is to risk a hardened heart (Heb 3:12–13). If we sense silence, our response must be repentance, not defiance. God still speaks today through his Word. Our call is to listen eagerly, obey fully, and never presume on his patience.

2. Sinful shortcuts deepen despair

Saul sought a medium at En-dor, grasping for answers outside of God's will. What seemed like a shortcut only deepened his despair. We face similar temptations—turning to worldly solutions, manipulative schemes, or ungodly counsel when God seems silent. Such shortcuts may promise relief but always bring ruin. The way forward is not around God but through him, in patient trust. Saul's tragic choice warns us that when God seems distant, we must draw near in repentance and faith, not chase substitutes. The only safe refuge is in God himself, whose wisdom never fails.

3. God's Word never fails

Samuel's prophecy of Saul's downfall came true with precision. Every word of God stands. This truth is both sobering and comforting. Sobering, because judgment will fall on those who reject him. Comforting, because his promises of grace are equally sure. We can trust his Word when it warns and when it comforts, when it convicts and when it assures. Saul's story reminds us that God's Word is not empty; it shapes history. Our response must be to build our lives on it, trusting that what God has spoken, he will surely accomplish.

4. Christ is the faithful King we need

The tragedy of Saul's kingship drives us to long for a better King. Saul fell in shame, disobedience, and despair. David, though flawed, pointed to another. Christ came as the true Anointed One, faithful in every way Saul was not. He never faltered, never rebelled, never sought forbidden counsel. Where Saul fell on Gilboa, Christ triumphed on Calvary, not by taking his own life but by giving it for ours. In him, despair turns to hope, judgment to mercy, and death to life. Saul's fall warns us, but Christ's victory secures us. He is the King who never fails, the Savior who reigns forever.

CONCLUSION

Firsat Samuel 28 and 31 close the book on Saul's tragic reign. His disobedience, desperation, and despair ended in silence, forbidden counsel, and death. Yet even in tragedy, God's word proved true. The contrast with David highlights the way of faith over fear, trust over rebellion. Ultimately, Saul's fall reminds us of the consequences of rejecting God's word and the hope of a faithful King. In Christ, we find the leader Saul never was—the One who listens to the Father, obeys fully, and secures victory for his people. Our call is to trust him, heed his Word, and live in the hope of his unfailing reign.

REFLECTION

1. Why did God remain silent when Saul inquired of him?
2. What was significant about Saul seeking the medium at En-dor?
3. How did Samuel's prophecy to Saul come true?
4. What does Saul's death reveal about rejecting God's Word?
5. How does Saul's tragedy point us to Christ as the faithful King?

DISCUSSION

1. What should we do when God seems silent in our lives?
2. What are some modern "shortcuts" we are tempted to pursue instead of trusting God?
3. How can we cultivate greater trust in God's Word?
4. What does Saul's fall teach us about leadership without faith?
5. How does Christ's victory on Calvary contrast with Saul's defeat on Gilboa?

www.ingramcontent.com/pod-product-compliance
Lightning Source LLC
Chambersburg PA
CBHW052122070526
44586CB00016B/2040